Never Nudge a Budgie!

100 Funny Poems
by
Colin West

WALKER BOOKS
AND SUBSIDIARIES
LONDON · BOSTON · SYDNEY · AUCKLAND

D0321013

Remember...

you can write a poem
on the back of an envelope,
in an old exercise book,
on a computer,
or in bed!
you can write a poem
on a piece of parchment,
in a classroom,
on a whim,
in a hurry,
on the bus,
or in your head!

Contents

When Betty Eats Spaghetti

When Betty eats spaghetti,
she slurps, she slurps, she slurps.
And when she's finished slurping,
she burps, she burps, she burps.

Freda, the Flat-footed Fairy

I'm Freda the flat-footed fairy,
my friends are the twinkle-toed lot –
they're slippery as butter,
they flit and they flutter
but look at these two feet *I've* got.

It's hard on a flat-footed fairy,
when others are nimble and quick,
to have two clodhoppers
which really are whoppers,
good only for giving a kick.

My friends are all frightfully flighty,
they frolic and fly fancy-free,
they're frothy and frilly
and frequently silly
and not at all clumsy like me.

My feet, like the lids of a dustbin,
are big and as flat as can be.
I can't be a leader,
I'm just poor old Freda,
the flat-footed fairy – that's me!

P.S. But wait! Things are not always awful
    and something that *does* make me laugh –
    I can stamp on a walnut,
    a big or a small nut,
    and break it quite cleanly in half!

Sir Hector

Sir Hector was a spectre
and he loved a lady ghost –
at midnight he'd collect her
and he'd drive her to the coast.

And there upon the shingle
they would rattle all their bones,
and ocean sounds would mingle
with their melancholy moans.

Percy the Pirate

When people think of pirates,
they think of strapping men
with cutlasses and whiskers,
and names like Jake or Ben.

But Percy was a pirate
more fearsome than the rest,
although he had no muscles
or hairs upon his chest.

For Percy's secret weapon
no brute could ever beat,
he never was without it –
his pair of smelly feet.

When he was out marauding,
his foes he would out-fox
by rapidly removing
his shoes, and then his socks.

Phew!

And then he'd do a handstand
and wave his feet aloft,
and so upon the ozone
the whiff would gently waft.

His victims' eyes would water,
their noses, they would sniff,
then fulsomely the fellows
would catch the pungent whiff.

And falling down like ninepins
they'd all be knocked out cold,
then Percy would relieve them
of jewellery and gold.

Yes, Percy was the pirate
no brute could ever beat,
who owned a ton of treasure
thanks solely to his feet.

My Obnoxious Brother Bobby

My obnoxious brother Bobby
has a most revolting hobby –
there behind the garden wall is
where he captures creepy-crawlies.

Grannies, aunts and baby cousins
come to our house in their dozens,
but they disappear discreetly
when they see him smiling sweetly.

For they know, as he approaches,
in his pockets are cockroaches,
spiders, centipedes and suchlike –
all of which they do not much like.

As they head towards the lobby,
bidding fond farewells to Bobby,
how they wish he'd change his habits
and keep guinea pigs or rabbits.

But their wishes are quite futile,
for he thinks that bugs are cute. I'll
finish now, but just remind you:
Bobby could be right behind you!

Norman Norton's Nostrils

Oh, Norman Norton's nostrils
are powerful and strong.
Hold on to your belongings,
if he should come along.

And do not ever let him
inhale with all his might,
or else your pens and pencils
will disappear from sight.

Right up his nose they'll vanish –
your future will be black.
Unless he gets the sneezes
you'll never get them back!

The Human cannonball

With a BANG as loud as thunder
a cannonball called Fred,
fast as a bolt of lightning,
goes zooming overhead.

Past startled swift and swallow, he hurtles on and on ...

till having reached his summit ...

h
e
p
l
u
m
m
e
t
s
l
i
k
e
a
s
t
o
n
e.

Then landing with a **WALLOP**,
head buried in the earth,
spectators, sixpence poorer,
have had their money's worth.

The Three chefs

Three chefs there were from Golders Green
(one tall, one small, one in-between),
who never could agree to what
exactly should go in the pot.

One widower, one bachelor,
one married man – a spatula,
an egg whisk and a rolling pin,
they'd use to do each other in.

They'd thrust, they'd wallop and they'd thump
until upon the floor they'd slump,
and there they'd most reluctantly
agree that they must disagree.

I wonder...

Laura
looks
a
little
like
a
lampstand.

Faye,
the
fairy
on
a
Christmas
tree.

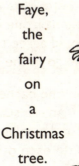

Alison
reminds
me
of
a
scarecrow.

I wonder, though, what people make of **ME!**

Granny's Greens

My granny grows the biggest veg
that I have ever seen.
There's no one in the whole wide world
whose fingers are so green.

She needs
massive pots
to grow her
shallots …

and cans
with huge
spouts
to water her
sprouts …

and
humongous
hoes
to tend her
bean rows …

and gigantic barrows
to carry her marrows...

Yes, Granny grows the biggest veg
that I have ever known –
and the balcony of Granny's flat
is where it all is grown!

In One Ear and Out the Other

When Miss Tibbs talks
to my dear brother,
it goes in one ear
and out the other.

And when she shouts
he seldom hears,
the words just whistle
through his ears.

His ears are big
(you must have seen 'em),
but he's got nothing
in between 'em.

The truth, Miss Tibbs,
is hard to face:
his head is full
of empty space.

Multiply 6 by 7, add 12 and

subtract

Tricky Tongue-twisters

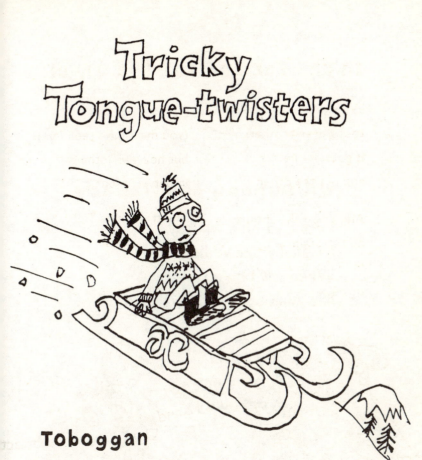

Toboggan

To begin to toboggan, first buy a toboggan,

but don't buy too big a toboggan.

(A too-big toboggan is not a toboggan

to buy to begin to toboggan.)

Willoughby the Wallaby

I want to be a wallaby,
a wallaby like Willoughby.
When *will* I be a wallaby
like Willoughby the wallaby?

When Jilly eats Jelly

When Jilly eats jelly,
then Jilly is jolly.
But melons make Melanie
most melancholy.

Canoe

I can't canoe my old canoe,
I need a new canoe.
Can you canoe my old canoe
and I'll canoe the new?

Adelaide

Adelaide is up a ladder.
Adelaide's an adder-upper.
She's an addled adder-upper,
adding adders up a ladder.

Juggler Jim

I'm Jim, and I juggle a jug and a jar,
and junkets and jelly and jam.
With jovial, joyful and jocular jests,
how jolly a jester I am!

Ethel Read a Book

Ethel read, Ethel read,

Ethel read a book.

Ethel read a book in bed,

she read a book on Ethelred.

The book that Ethel read in bed

(the book on Ethelred) was red.

The book was red that Ethel read

in bed on Ethelred.

Nutpickers

Who nicked the nuts
that the nutpickers picked
when the nutpickers
picked their nuts?

The picnickers nicked
the nutpickers' nuts
when the nutpickers
picked their nuts.

The Backpacker's Picnic

A backpacker packing a picnic
picked up his backpack to pack.

He popped in a pippin,
a pork pie, some pickle,
a packet of peanuts
and pineapple pop.

With picnic now packed up,
the backpacker picked up
his backpack to put on his back.

Passers-by

A passer-by was passing by a by-pass,

and passing by the by-pass,

a passer-by passed by.

By passing by a by-pass

as a passer-by passed by,

a passer-by was passed by

by a by-pass passer-by.

What do Teachers Dream of?

What do teachers dream of,

in mountains and in lowlands?

They dream of exclamation marks,

full stops and semi-colons!

The Baby's Lament

When Mum puts on
my nappy tight,
I somehow lose
my appetite!

My Hairstyle

My hairstyle
is a rare style:
a crop
on top,
a quiff
sprayed stiff,
the left side
I've dyed
snowy white,
while the right
is the blackest of black
and a ponytail
hangs at the back!

My cat

My cat's so much a mass of fur,

I'm not sure if it's him or her.

Orange, Silver, Sausage

Some words I've studied for a time,

like orange, silver, sausage –

but as for finding them a rhyme,

I'm at a total lossage.

My Auntie

My auntie who lives in
Llanfairpwllgwyngyllgogerych-
    wyrndrobwllllantysiliogogogoch
has asked me to stay.

But unfortunately
Llanfairpwllgwyngyllgogerych-
    wyrndrobwllllantysiliogogogoch
is a long, long way away.

Will I ever go to
Llanfairpwllgwyngyllgogerych-
    wyrndrobwllllantysiliogogogoch?
It's difficult to say.

Bed of Nails

I sleep upon a bed of nails.
I must confess, it never fails
to help me get a good night's rest,
and, overall, I'm most impressed!

Never Nudge a Budgie!

O, never nudge a budgie
if a budgie will not budge.
A budgie's not for nudging
and a budgie bears a grudge
against anybody nudging him,
so around him you must trudge.
For budgies aren't for budging,
so a budgie never nudge!

Trampoline

I've got a hundred pounds to spend, and I am really keen,

if you would only serve me, Miss, to buy this trampoline.

I'm sorry to disturb you, Miss, I hate to intervene,

but could you for a moment, please, put down your magazine?

PLEASE PAY HERE

£99.99

Riding to School

I wouldn't half laugh if I saw a giraffe

riding to school on a scooter,

and even more funny would be a big bunny

following, honking his hooter.

Rolling Down a Hill

I'm rolling
rolling
rolling
down,

I'm rolling
down a
hill.

I'm rolling
rolling
rolling
down,

I'm rolling
down it
still.

I'm rolling
rolling
down.

I'm rolling
down a
hill.

I'm rolling
rolling
rolling
down,

but now
I'm feeling
ill.

chopping Off Granny's Head

I've gone and chopped off Granny's head

and cut Grandad in half –

I really must learn how to take

a better photograph!

Adolphus

Adolphus is despicable –

before the day begins,

to prove that I am kickable,

he kicks me in the shins.

The Wherefore and the Why

The Therefore and the Thereupon,
the Wherefore and the Why,
the Hitherto, the Whitherto,
the Thus, the Thence, the Thy.

The Whysoever, Whereupon,
the Whatsoever, Whence,
the Hereinafter, Hereupon,
the Herebefore and Hence.

The Thereby and the Thereabouts,
the Thee, the Thou, the Thine –
I don't care for their whereabouts,
and they don't care for mine!

To Be a Bee?

To be a bee or not to be
a bee, that is the question.
You see, I'm in a quandary.
To be a bee or not to be
a bee is what perplexes me –
pray, what is your suggestion?
To be a bee or not to be
a bee, that is the question.

An Understanding Man

I have an understanding
with an understanding man:
his umbrella I stand under
when I understand I can.

Bubblegum

Bubblegum is troublesome

when stuck upon your sole.

Tread carefully and prayerfully

if going for a stroll.

Dodgems

I put
my foot
down
really
HARD

when I drive a dodgem car

and off I go
(I'm
never
slow)

I feel
like I'm
a star!

I twist and spin the car I'm in

round corners really tight

and
other
cars
caught
in a
jam

**I RAM
WITH ALL
MY MIGHT!**

Pogo Stick

Upon my pogo stick I pounce

and out of school I homeward bounce.

I bounce so high, how my heart pounds,

until at last I'm out of bounds.

Vicious Verses

Sidney

He ate up all the pies, did Sidney,

then sadly, he EXPLODED, didn't he?

The pitch, no mistake,

was spattered with steak,

and the stands were all covered with kidney.

Double Trouble

Pray spare a thought for Connie Cook

whose nose was always in a book.

She'd still be here amongst us if

she hadn't walked so near a cliff.

Remember also Philip Fox

whose hobby was collecting rocks –

if Connie hadn't squashed him flat,

he'd be here too and not gone splat!

coat hanger

I gave my love a coat hanger.

She flung it back at me.

It acted like a boomerang, and hit her on the knee.

cousin Jane

Yesterday my cousin Jane
said she was an aeroplane,
but I wanted further proof –

so I pushed her off the roof.

Aunt carol

Making vinegar, Aunt Carol
fell into her brimming barrel.
As she drowned, my teardrops trickled –
now she's permanently pickled.

Laurence

Laurence by a lion was mauled,
and it's left us quite appalled.
He had on his Sunday best –
now he's gone and torn his vest.

When Rover Passed Over

When Rover died, my sister cried.
I tried my best to calm her.
I said, "We'll have him mummified,
I know a good embalmer."

And so we packed the wretched pup
into a wicker basket.
We duly had him bandaged up,
and kept him in a casket.

Now Rover we will not forget,
though he is but a dummy,
for though we've lost a faithful pet,
we've gained an extra mummy!

Kitty

Isn't it a
dreadful pity
what became of
dreamy Kitty,
noticing the
moon above her,
not the
    missing
       manhole
         cover?

Auntie Babs

Auntie Babs became besotted

with her snake, so nicely spotted,

unaware that pets so mottled

like to leave their keepers throttled.

An ABC of Tragedy

A was an Archer
who filled me with fear

B was a Barber
who cut off my ear

C was a Chemist
who poisoned my tea

D was a Doctor
who hammered my knee

E was an Electrician
who gave me a shock

F was a Fighter
who knocked off my block

G was a Ghostie –
or was it a Ghoul?

H was a Headmaster
who called me a fool

I was an Infant
who made me feel sick

J was a Jester
who gave me a kick

K was a King
who was bad as can be

L was a Lumberjack
whose tree fell on me

M was a Magician
who sawed me in two

N was a Nutcase
who lived in my loo

O was an Oarsman
in whose boat I sank

P was a Pirate
who said, "Walk the plank!"

Q was a Queen and
she chopped off my head

R was a Robber
who filled me with lead

S was a Stranger
who stole all he could

T was a Tailor
who stitched me up good

U was a Unicyclist
who knocked me down flat

V was a Villain
who kidnapped my cat

W was a Werewolf
who had awful breath

and X, Y and Z,
they just bored me to death

Little Barbara

Little Barbara went to Scarborough,

just to buy a candelabra.

At the harbour, a bear ate Barbara.

Don't you find that most macabre?

The Greedy Alligator

I have a rather greedy pet,
a little alligator.
When he my younger sister met,
he opened wide and ate her.

But soon he learned that he was wrong
to eat the child in question,
for he felt bad before too long,
and suffered indigestion.

This story seems to prove to me
that he who rudely gobbles
will soon regret his gluttony
and get the collywobbles.

Auntie Dotty

My Auntie Dotty thought it nice
to twirl about upon the ice.
I warned her persons of proportions
such as hers should take precautions.
But poor Aunt Dotty was so fond
of skating on the village pond
that she took no heed of warning
and went skating every morning.

Now we mourn for Auntie Dot:
the ice was thin, but she was not.

Nothing but Nonsense

Funny Bone

It's true I have a funny bone

(we all have, I believe),

it's just that I don't show it off,

I keep it up my sleeve.

Falling Flat

In Norfolk alone in a cornfield,
a ruminative fellow once sat,
surveying that rather forlorn field
and noticing how it was flat.

"When I were a nipper," he pondered,
"we'd always a hillock or two,
and ranges wherever we wandered
with peaks like the ones in Peru.

We'd cliffs and we'd crags and we'd mountains,
of flatness there wasn't a trace.
We'd spouting volcanoes and fountains
and ridges all over the place."

The fellow then rose from his hummock,
but, all of a sudden, he slipped,
and soon he was flat on his stomach,
as over a molehill he'd tripped.

Jocelyn, My Dragon

My dragon's name is Jocelyn,
he's something of a joke.
For Jocelyn is very tame,
he doesn't like to maul or maim
or breathe a fearsome fiery flame —
he's much too smart to smoke.

And when I take him to the park
the children form a queue,
and say, "What lovely eyes of red!"
as one by one they pat his head.
And Jocelyn is so well-bred,
he only eats a few!

The Flipper-Flopper Bird

O have you never ever heard
of the Flipper-Flopper Bird?
O have you never seen his teeth,
two above and one beneath?

O have you never known the thrill
of stroking his enormous bill?
O have you never taken tea
with him sitting up a tree?

O have you never seen him hop
as he goes a-flip, a-flop?
O have you never heard his cry?
No, you've never? Nor have I.

The Ogglewop

The Ogglewop is tall and wide
and though he looks quite passive,
he's crammed with boys and girls inside –
that's why he is so massive!

The Darkest and Dingiest Dungeon

Down in the darkest and dingiest dungeon,
far from the tiniest twinkle of stars,
far from the whiff of a wonderful luncheon,
far from the murmur of motoring cars,
far from the habits of rabbits and weasels,
far from the merits of ferrets and stoats,
far from the danger of mumps or of measles,
far from the fashions of fabulous coats,

far from the turn of a screw in a socket,
far from the fresh frozen food in the fridge,
far from the fluff in my duffle coat pocket,
far from the bite of a mischievous midge,
far from the hole in my humble umbrella,
far from my hat as it hangs in the hall,
I sit here alone with myself in the cellar,
I do so like getting away from it all!

The Blunderblat

Until I saw the Blunderblat
I doubted its existence –
but late last night with Vera White
I saw one in the distance.

I reached for my binoculars,
which finally I focused –
I watched it rise into the skies
like some colossal locust.

I heard it hover overhead,
I shrieked as it came nearer –
I held my breath, half-scared to death,
and prayed it might take Vera.

And so it did, I'm glad to say,
without too much resistance –
dear Blunderblat, I'm sorry that
I doubted your existence.

The Gobblegulp

The Gobblegulp is most uncouth.
In his mouth is just one tooth.
He gobbles food and gulps Ribena
like a living vacuum cleaner.
He has a great big bulging belly
that wobbles when he walks like jelly,
but what I like about him least
is that he is a noisy beast,
for when he eats an apple crumble,
his tummy starts to roll and rumble –
I often hear a noise and wonder,
"Was that a Gobblegulp or thunder?"

cats and Dogs

Would you rather have a moggy than a doggy?
Would you rather hear a purr than hear a yap?
Would you rather stroke a feline than a canine?
Would you rather have a cat upon your lap?

OR

Would you rather have a "Towser" than a mouser?
Would you rather go for walks than stay at home?
Would you rather hear a bowwow than a miaow?
Would you rather have a dog who likes to roam?

My Pterodactyl

Once I had a pterodactyl
and I kept him in a shack till
he escaped. Alas, alack! Till
he comes back, my world is black. Till
then with pain I shall be racked, till
he comes back, my pterodactyl.

New Nursery Rhyme

Hey diddle diddle,

the cat smashed the fiddle.

The cow pulled a face

at the moon.

The little dog snored

because he was bored

and the dish had a fight

with the spoon.

A Crocodile's Teeth

A crocodile's teeth are a problem,
a crocodile's teeth are a pain.
A crocodile suffers the toothache
again and again and again.

Now, getting the toothache so often
makes crocodiles lose all their bite,
and desperate measures are called for
to bring back their lost appetite.

Thus crocodiles go to the dentist,
on average, every eight years.
(Quite by chance that's precisely how often
a dentist, somewhere, disappears.)

Me and Amanda

Me
and
Amanda
meander,
like
rivers
that
run
to
the
sea.

We
wander
at
random,
we're
always
in
tandem:
meandering
Mandy
and
me!

Ben

Ben's done something really bad,
he's forged a letter from his dad:

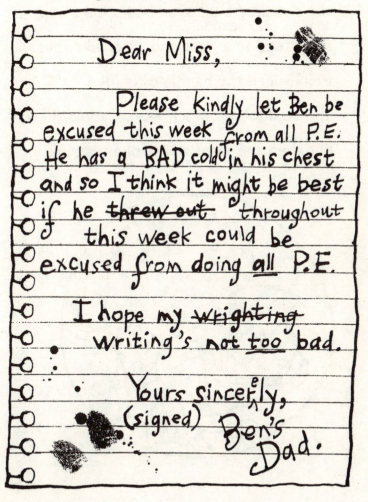

Dear Miss,

Please kindly let Ben be
excused this week from all P.E.
He has a BAD cold in his chest
and so I think it might be best
if he ~~threw out~~ throughout
this week could be
excused from doing all P.E.

I hope my ~~wrighting~~
writing's not too bad.

Yours sincerely,
(signed) Ben's
Dad.

clumsy clarissa

Clarissa did the washing up:

she smashed a plate and chipped a cup

and dropped a glass and cracked a mug,

then pulled the handle off a jug.

She couldn't do much worse, you'd think,

but then she went and broke the sink.

Curious Creatures

Stan the Goldfish

I have a goldfish, name of Stan,

who has a short attention span:

so short that when you call his name,

he comes, then wonders why he came.

Auntie Agnes's cat

My Auntie Agnes has a cat.
I do not like to tell her that
its body seems a little large
(with lots of stripes for camouflage).
Its teeth and claws are also larger
than they ought to be. A rajah
gave her the kitten, I recall,
when she was stationed in Bengal.
But that was many years ago,
and kittens are inclined to grow.
So now she has a fearsome cat –
but I don't like to tell her that.

The orang-utan

The closest relative of man,

they say, is the orang-utan –

and when I look at Grandpapa,

I realise how right they are.

Octopus

Last Saturday I came across
a rather laid-back octopus.
I couldn't help but make a fuss,
and shook him by the tentacle.

He seemed to find it all a bore
and asked me, "Have we met before?
I'm sorry, but I can't be sure.
You chaps all look identical."

Moose

What use
a moose?

Except, perhaps,
for coats and caps.

Our Hippopotamus

We thought a lively pet to keep
might be a hippopotamus.
Now see him sitting in a heap
and notice, at the bottom, us.

Good Homes for Kittens

Who'd like a Siamese?
Yes, please.

An Angora?
I'd adora.

A Black and White?
All right.

A Tortoiseshell?
Oh, very well.

A Manx?
No thanx!

Geraldine Giraffe

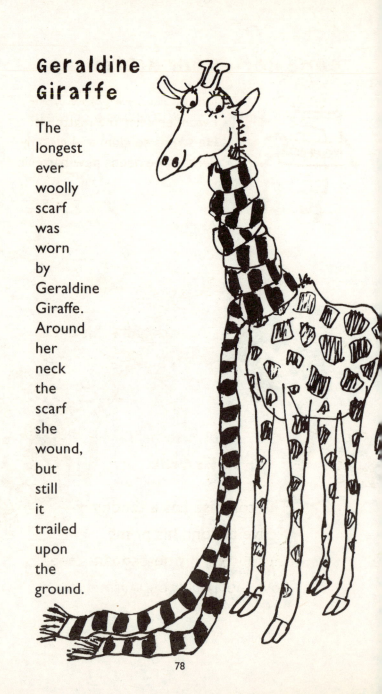

The
longest
ever
woolly
scarf
was
worn
by
Geraldine
Giraffe.
Around
her
neck
the
scarf
she
wound,
but
still
it
trailed
upon
the
ground.

Glow-worm

I know a worried glow-worm.
I wonder what the matter is?
He seems so glum and gloomy.
Perhaps he needs new batteries!

The Tortoise

The tortoise has a tendency
to live beyond his prime,
thus letting his descendants see
how they will look in time.

chameleons

Chameleons are seldom seen.
They're red, they're orange, then they're green.
They're one of nature's strangest sights –
their colours change like traffic lights!

Anteater

Pray, have you met my nice new pet?
An anteater is he.
There's just one hitch – I'm apt to itch
when serving up his tea.

The sloth

The sloth may smile,
the sloth may frown.
It's hard to tell —
he's upside down!

Proboscis monkey

Proboscis monkey, I suppose
you've grown accustomed to your nose.
But what precisely did you do
to get that nose to grow on you?

The Pig

The table manners of the pig
leave much to be desired.
His appetite is always big,
his talk is uninspired.

And if you ask him out to dine
you'll only ask him once,
unless you like to see a swine
who gobbles as he grunts.

Ridiculous Rhymes

Insides

I'm very grateful to my skin
for keeping all my insides in –
I do so hate to think about
what I would look like inside out.

The Stand-offish cat

A stand-offish cat
once sat on the mat,
and this is the thought
that came as he sat:
"This isn't the place
I should truly be at,
for I'm far from being
a sit-downish cat."
So that stand-offish cat
got up off the mat
and never sat down
on the mat
after that!

Love Song

I tried to serenade my love
but couldn't sing a single note –
and all because of a FROG!
(A frog in my throat.)

So I wrote a letter to my love –
but the outcome, too, was crummy.
I dared not post it because of BUTTERFLIES!
(Butterflies in my tummy.)

I thought then an artistic dance
might demonstrate romance,
but it all went wrong because of ANTS!
(Ants in my pants.)

At last I wrote a little ode
to show my love so dear ...
but she sent me away with a FLEA!
(A flea in my ear.)

Socks

My local Gents' Outfitter stocks
the latest line in snazzy socks:
black socks, white socks,
morning, noon and night socks,
grey socks, green socks,
small, large and in-between socks,
blue socks, brown socks,
always-falling-down socks,
orange socks, red socks,
baby socks and bed socks,
purple socks, pink socks,
what-would-people-think socks,
holey socks and frayed socks,
British Empire-made socks,
long socks, short socks,
any-sort-of-sport socks,
thick socks, thin socks,
and "these-have-just-come-in" socks.

Socks with stripes and socks with spots,
socks with stars and polka dots,
socks for ankles, socks for knees,
socks with twelve-month guarantees,
socks for aunties, socks for uncles,
socks to cure you of carbuncles,
socks for nephews, socks for nieces,
socks that won't show up their creases,
socks whose colour glows fluorescent,
socks for child or adolescent,
socks for ladies, socks for gents,
socks for only fifty pence...

Socks for winter, socks for autumn,
socks with garters to support 'em,
socks for work and socks for leisure,
socks hand-knitted, made-to-measure,
socks of wool and polyester,
socks from Lincoln, Leeds and Leicester,
socks of cotton and elastic,
socks of paper, socks of plastic,
socks of silk-embroidered satin,
socks with mottoes done in Latin,
socks for soldiers in the army,
socks to crochet or macramé,
socks for destinations distant,
shrink-proof, stretch-proof, heat-resistant.

Baggy socks, brief socks,
Union Jack motif socks,
chequered socks, tartan socks,
school or kindergarten socks,
sensible socks, silly socks,
frivolous and frilly socks,
impractical socks, impossible socks,
drip-dry machine-only-washable socks,
Bulgarian socks, Brazilian socks,
there seem to be over a million socks!

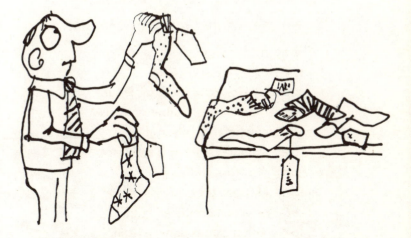

With all these socks, there's just one catch –
it's hard to find a pair that match.

Annie and her Anaconda

Annie and her anaconda
wander near and wander yonder.
When they wander here, I wonder
whether Annie's anaconda
likes it here – or is he fonder
of the far-off places yonder?
Where I wish I were, I ponder.
'Scuse me, while I grab my Honda!

Hedgehog's Valentine

If you're sickly,
feeling prickly,
as your trickly
tears fall thickly,
don't act fickly,
kiss me quickly,
you'll feel tickly,
not so prickly
and partickly
far from sickly.

Knitting

She tried to knit a nightcap,
she tried to knit a scarf,
she tried to knit a cardigan:
too big they were, by half.

She tried to knit a waistcoat,
she tried to knit a shawl,
she tried to knit a bobble hat:
they all turned out too small.

And now she's knitting knickers
and if they do not fit,
we'll make her wear them anyhow
until she's learnt to knit.

Joe

We don't mention Joe
in this house any more.
No, not since he nailed
Mother's boots to the floor.
What makes matters worse
with regard to this crime
is Mother was wearing
her boots at the time.

The Lighthouse Keeper

I met the lighthouse
keeper's wife,
his nephew, niece,
and daughter –
his uncle and his
auntie too,
when I went across
the water.

I met the lighthouse
keeper's son,
his father and his
mother –
his grandpa and his
grandma too,
his sister and his
brother.

I met the lighthouse
keeper's mate,
who, running out
of patience,
told me, "The keeper's
gone ashore
to round up more
relations."

Llulu and her Llama

Lluckless Llulu's llost her llittle llama,
her llovely llittle llama known as Llen:
Llulu llast had Llen at Lluton
(Llulu lleft him in Lleft Lluggage),
but it llooks llike Llulu won't see Llen again!

Some clothes

Some clothes are in the cupboard.
But there's one thing for sure:
raincoats, frocks and dresses
aren't what I'm looking for.

Some clothes are in the cupboard,
and some are in the drawer.
But knickers, vests and hankies
aren't what I'm looking for.

Some clothes are in the cupboard,
and some are in a drawer,
and some are hanging on a hook
upon my bedroom door.
But a nightie and a dressing gown
aren't what I'm looking for.

Some clothes are in the cupboard,
and some are in a drawer,
and some are hanging on a hook
upon my bedroom door,
and some are lying on my bed,
and underneath are more.
But slippers, shoes and sandals
aren't what I'm looking for.

Some clothes are in the cupboard,
and some are in a drawer,
and some are hanging on a hook
upon my bedroom door,
and some are lying on my bed,
and underneath are more,
and some are even piled in heaps
which cover all the floor.

Yippee! My witch's outfit!
That's what I'm looking for!

Leaflets

Leaflets, leaflets, I like leaflets,
I love leaflets when they're free.
When I see a pile of leaflets,
I take one or two (or three).

Banks are always good for leaflets –
they've got lots of leaflets there.
Leaflets on investing money:
How to be a Millionaire.

And I go to my sports centre,
for their leaflets are such fun,
and I visit travel agents –
they've got leaflets by the ton.

Leaflets, leaflets, I like leaflets,
I love leaflets when they're free.
When I see a pile of leaflets,
something strange comes over me.

Theatre foyers offer leaflets:
What to See and How to Book.
Stations, libraries and so on –
all have leaflets if you look.

I've got leaflets by the dozen,
I've got leaflets by the score,
I've got leaflets by the hundred,
yet I always yearn for more.

Adrian

Has everyone met Adrian?
He really is a hoot.
I gave a birthday party –
so he wore his birthday suit.

And when he played his trumpet
it was wonderful to hear –
he didn't put it to his lips
but played the thing by ear.

And then he babysat for us
and acted just as daft:
he sat upon the baby
and he laughed and laughed
and laughed.

O, if you should meet Adrian
and say, "How do you do?"
"How do I do precisely what?"
is what he'll ask of you.

Sports

Playing tennis,
I'm no menace.
As for croquet,
I'm just OK.

Then there's cricket –
can't quite lick it.
Ditto rowing,
discus throwing.

Also biking,
jogging, hiking,
ten-pin bowling
and pot-holing.

Can't play hockey,
I'm no jockey.
Daren't go riding
or hang-gliding.

Nor can I jump
long or high jump.
Being sporty
ain't my forté.

I'm pathetic,
un-athletic,
but at dinner ...
I'm a winner!

wallabagoo

I'm glad that I live here in Wallabagoo,
there's always a zillion things you can do –
you can lie in the shade of a Tippety Tree
and watch as a Bottle Bee lands on your knee.
You can sip a Zonata or nibble a Nog
or hear the far call of the wild Jitterjog.

It's better than living in Mumble-on-Murk,
for when you live there, all you do is hard work.
There are Fiskets to fill up and Coggles to turn
and seventeen Scrudles a year's all you earn.
Yes, happy am I here in Wallabagoo.
I bet that you'd like to be living here too!

The Walrus who Worried

There once was a walrus who worried.
He worried of this and of that.
He worried he'd fall off the edge of the world
if the world wasn't round, but was flat.

He worried the sky would fall on him,
he worried the sea would go dry,
he worried that if he went out for a walk,
he'd vanish and never know why.

He worried so much and so often,
he worried himself inside out.
Then having done that, what then worried him most –
he'd nothing to worry about.

Practical Joker

I used to spend my pocket money
on things I thought funny:

exploding pens,
life-like slugs,
jump-apart toffees,
joke bedbugs,
a whoopee cushion,
a flower that squirts,
an electric shock book
(that really hurts!),
a rubber kipper,
some plastic chocs
and non-strike matches
in a box.

I thought I was a funny bloke,
but others never saw the joke!